# The Sunday Post

### PRINTED AND PUBLISHED IN GLASGOW EVERY SUNDAY MORNING.

**Morning Special**

NO. 1593. [ REGISTERED AT THE GENERAL POST OFFICE AS A NEWSPAPER. ] SUNDAY, MARCH 8, 1936. PRICE TWOPENCE

# EUROPE ALARMED

VIEWS OF COLOGNE AND FRANKFURT IN THE DEMILITARISED RHINELAND ZONE, WHICH COMPRISES THE LEFT BANK OF THE RHINE, AND A 50-KILOMETRE STRIP OF THE RIGHT BANK. THE ZONE INCLUDES AIX-LA-CHAPELLE, TRIER, THE ARMAMENTS CITY OF ESSEN, AND THE SAAR.

## FRANCE'S RETORT TO HITLER'S MOVE

## ALL ARMY LEAVE CANCELLED

### Mr Eden Confers With Premier : Rhineland's Great Welcome to "Goose-steppers"

Every Capital in Europe is seething with excitement following Hitler's denunciation of the Locarno Treaty, and the dramatic march of German troops into the demilitarised Rhineland zone.

France is particularly perturbed, and Paris simply astounded by the suddenness of the march.

Although Hitler threatened such a move as Germany's reply to the signing of the Franco-Soviet Pact, France never imagined that German troops would move so swiftly.

France will appeal to the League demanding action against Germany under the Locarno Pact and the League Covenant.

Week-end leave for part of the French army has been cancelled. The Rhineland frontier fortifications were the scene of extensive troop movements a fortnight ago, skeleton forces manning the underground frontier fortresses being increased by drafts of troops from the interior.

The Belgian Government cancelled all leave for the troops in the garrisons on the eastern frontiers.

Not only will Britain, Italy and Belgium hear from M. Flandin immediately what France thinks of the move, but M. Flandin is calling a meeting of the allies of France—Russia, Czechoslovakia, Jugo-Slavia, and Rumania—to take place within the next few hours.

The German Ambassador, Herr Von Hoesch, called at the British Foreign Office in London yesterday, and left with Mr Anthony Eden, the Foreign Secretary, the German memorandum about the denunciation of the Locarno Treaty.

### MR EDEN SEES PREMIER

Mr Anthony Eden, after seeing French, Belgian, and Italian Ambassadors in London, hurried to Chequers, and had a long talk with Mr Baldwin.

The Cabinet will discuss the situation at a special meeting called for Monday. To-night in well-informed diplomatic circles it is stated British Ministers take the view the situation is very serious, but there is no need for panic.

Mr Eden saw the German Ambassador on Friday afternoon, and told him, with the prior knowledge of the French Government, that Britain was anxious to enter into discussions for a western Air Pact.

Herr Von Hoesch took note of this representation, but no indication was given of Germany's attitude at that time.

The British Government had no knowledge when Mr Eden saw Herr Von Hoesch on Friday of the nature of the German declaration made yesterday.

### FINANCIAL SLUMP IN VIENNA

In Vienna Hitler's speech caused the gravest anxiety in financial circles. A great slump set in immediately in the stock market.

In Rome Germany's offer to re-enter the League has caused astonishment.

The first reaction is one of satisfaction. It is generally felt that the League is too much under the domination of Great Britain and France, and that the return of Germany will provide a useful counter-balancing force.

### MOSCOW IS SCEPTICAL

Herr Hitler's address to the Reichstag is regarded in Moscow as a hopeless shriek in view of the impending ratification of the Franco-Soviet Pact by the French Senate.

His offer to re-enter the League is regarded as a joke savouring of impudence. The suggestion that France should abandon border fortresses in favour of demilitarised zones is viewed as absurd.

Great excitement was caused in Brussels when the news became known. A special meeting of the Cabinet has been called for Monday.

Geneva regards Hitler's memorandum as one of the most statesman-like proposals that have ever emerged from any European Chancellery.

The offer to return to the League disarms the French Government, which has always made this a preliminary consideration to any rapprochement with Germany.

Washington views the German move is fraught with grave possibilities, and constitutes a direct challenge to France.

### GERMAN SOLDIERS FETED IN RHINE TOWNS

To-night, Cologne, Coblenz, Frankfurt, and Mainz, with all the old fortresses reoccupied, were feting the goose-stepping soldiers.

The Lord Mayor of Cologne personally welcomed the soldiers as they poured across the forbidden bridge to the western side of the river, and the Council members had decked the streets with laurels.

## What Hitler Proposes To Do

When the German Foreign Minister, Baron von Neurath, met the Ambassadors of Great Britain, France, Italy, and Belgium yesterday, he handed them a note and announced that a battalions of German troops marched into the Rhineland at noon.

This was described to the Ambassadors as a kind of demonstration done as unostentatiously as possible.

Whilst Hitler was speaking in the Reichstag, troops were marching into Mainz, Coblence, Cologne, and Frankfort.

Garrisons were being re-occupied and so were former fortresses.

Troops also marched into Deutz, opposite Cologne, while military planes flew overhead.

Events moved swiftly and dramatically.

Hitler suddenly convened the Reichstag to hear a declaration of the Government.

### Germany's Offer

Handed to the Ambassadors an hour earlier are points in the Note:—

1. Germany is ready to establish with France and Belgium mutual demilitarised zones on either side of the frontier as deep as those countries desire.

2. Germany is ready to conclude a non-aggression pact with France and Belgium, suggesting 25 years as a satisfactory period for this.

3. Germany invites Britain and Italy to become guarantors of the non-aggression pact with France and Belgium.

4. Holland might join this pact if she so desired, and the other Powers considered it opportune.

5. Without specifying which Powers should sign it, Germany reiterates the

previous suggestion of an air pact designed to avoid unprovoked air attacks.

6. Germany expresses her willingness to conclude a non-aggression pact with all states bordering her on the east, including Lithuania, in view of that country's changed attitude on the Memel question.

7. Germany is willing to return to the League of Nations, but the Covenant must be separate from the Versailles Treaty.

*Hitler's Speech—See Back Page.*

## Barrier Collapses At Aberdeen

### Crowd's Mistake Thrilling Game

Ninety-seven thousand people paid £3954 to see the four round Scottish Cup ties yesterday at Glasgow, Aberdeen, Greenock and Falkirk.

Attraction No. 1 was the Aberdeen-Rangers game at Pittodrie. The crowd of 41,663 was a record.

A last-minute goal by Turnbull gave Rangers victory. It was a real golden goal, worth with £1000 to Ibrox.

During one of the thrilling moments a barrier in the she fund enclosure collapsed. Two were injured.

An extraordinary incident occurred in the closing minutes of the match. hundreds of spectators swarmed on the field under the impression the game was finished.

They were not wholly to blame for their mistake. Everyone of that crowd must have heard their own thumping, for the match was a thriller.

Turnbull put a corner behind, when Referee Martin blew his whistle just a trifle too long the crowd thought the game was over.

There was an ominous swaying at the sea end, where the embankment Policemen into the crowd, and, their brawn into it, managed to ease the swaying temporarily.

During one of the exciting moments of the game the swaying started once more at the sea end. the mass swung forward one of the barriers on the terraces collapsed. Men and women fell in a heap. Thomas M'Kay, Motherwell Loan deen, was seriously injured.

*Wireless Programmes*

---

The headline of The Sunday Post on March 8, 1936 was a sombre one as Britain moved inexorably towards war. But this issue marked the beginning of something much less sombre with the introduction of Oor Wullie and The Broons in the Sunday Post Fun Section. These strips have become national treasures and this book contains a selection of iconic and rarely seen strips from the early years.

SUPPLEMENT TO THE SUNDAY POST, MARCH 8 1936.

**EVER HEARD OF THESE PEOPLE?**
May Pole.
Maggie Zene.
Mary Christmas.
Mike Rophone.
Violet Ray.
Ben E. Diction.
Chris Anthemum.
Dick Tionary.
Ed Ucation.

**SOME FAMOUS MACS.**
—intosh.
—aroni.
—(s)welltown Braes.
—connachie.
—no difference.
—beth.
—aroon.
—merry.
tar—

**DO YOU KNOW?**
Time flies.
Wine vaults.
Grass slopes.
Music stands.
Niagara falls.
Moonlight walks.
Kent hops.
Holiday trips.
Indiarubber tyres.
The organ stops.
Trade returns.
Marble busts.

Teacher—" What is the plural of ' child ' ?"
Tommy—" Twins."

" When you and your brother fight, who usually wins ?"
" Father."

---

**TEN TIPS.**
" What is the secret of success?"
" Push," said the Button.
" Never be lead," said the Pencil.
" Take pains," said the Window.
" Always keep cool," said the Ice.
" Be up-to-date," said the Calendar.
" Never lose your head," said the Match.
" Make light of your troubles," said the Fire.
" Do a driving business," said the Hammer.
" Stick to it," said the Gluepot.
" Don't get rattled," said the old Tin Lizzie.

Little Boy—" How deep is it in the middle, mister "
Bather—" Oh, about up to my chin."
Little Boy — " Which chin?"

Johnny—" Look at the rhinoceros."
Willie—" That ain't no rhinoceros, that's a hippopotamus. Can't you see it hasn't got a radiator cap ?"

Waiter—" Hungary ?"
Diner—" Yes, Siam."
Waiter—" Right, I'll Fiji."

Teacher—" What is the largest ant you have ever heard of ?"
Tommy—" The eleph-ant."

City Chap (pointing at haystack)—" What kind of a house is that?"
Country Ditto—" That's not a house, that's hay."
City Chap — " Go on. You can't fool me. Hay doesn't grow in a lump like that!"

---

**DON'T YOU BELIEVE IT.**
A black hen lays black and white eggs in April.
Macaroni was originally used by the Romans as pea-shooters.
In 1800 the Australian Cricket team beat Arsenal in the final of the Cup by two lengths and a short head.
Cricket balls were once square and made of dough. They were called doughballs.
An African bird called the Toocatoo flies backwards, so that it will remember where it has come from.
A snail has asbestos-lined brakes.
At Usqubash, in Iceland, Walter Lindrum compiled a break of 113,114, and was then disqualified for failing to replace the turf.

Man in Water—" Help!"
Jew (holding up lifebelt) —" How much for this "

**SHORT AND SWEET.**

| Smart. | Sharp. |
| --- | --- |
| Going ? | Where ? |
| Carnival. | To-night ? |
| Yes. | No ! |
| Should. | Why ? |
| Jolly. | Perhaps. |
| Fun. | Rotten. |
| Pessimist ? | Mebbe. |
| Why ? | Worried. |
| Headache ? | No. |
| Toothache ? | No. |
| What ? | Broke ! |

**CHEESY !**
Heboltsasandwichandsome cheese,
Apieceortwoofpie,
Andgulpsacupofcoffeedown,
Whileyoucanwinkaneye.

And later on there comes to him,
A very common question.
He wonders how it was that he
Contracted indigestion.

Circus Manager — " What's wrong now ?"
Indiarubber Man — " Every time the strong man writes a letter he uses me to rub out the mistakes."

---

**OUR ADVERT. DEPARTMENT.**

**Anything You Like You Can Get Here.**

Wanted.—A grand piano for a lady with four wooden legs.
For Sale.—Fox terrier and kennel with pedigree.
Cricket pitch wanted by cricketers twenty-eight yard long and twenty-five yards broad.
The Whackem Carpet-Cleaning Factory.—Send your carpets to us. Don't kill your wife. Let us do your dirty work.
For Sale.—Car 1910 model. Only requires overhauling. Owner willing to exchange for roller skates.
Boy. — Willing, energetic, athletic, wishes job. Anything considered, but would prefer job counting spots in domino factory.
For Sale.—Football, match size. Only requires new bladder and outer cover. Lace in good condition.

Breathes there a man with soul so dead,
Who never to himself has said,
As he banged his toe against the bed—
" !!!! ????? !!!! ??? !!?"

Budge—" Why has he got two horses ?"
Jim—" That's in case one gets punctured."

Teacher—" Now, Andy, give me a sentence with ' seldom.' "
Andy—" My father had two goats, and he ' seldom.' "

Pat—" If I'm up first I'll put a chalk mark on this post."
Mick—" An' if I'm up before you I'll rub it off."

Tom—" What's a mermaid ?"
Dick—" Half a flapper, and half a kipper."

Teacher (to small boy) — " Spell what you wipe your nose on."
Small Boy—" S-l-e-e-v-e."

---

An Indian wished to send the news of his mother's death to an English friend. This was what he wrote—" The hand that rocked the cradle has kicked the bucket."

Upon the Persian borders
Stood a Russian ill at ease;
Mused he, " Do I hear orders,
Or did the General sneeze?"

**A FAMILY HEIRLOOM.**
When dad has worn his trousers out,
They pass to brother John ;
Then mother turns them round about,
And Willie puts them on.

When Willie's legs too long have grown,
The trousers fail to hide them,
So Jimmy claims them for his own,
And stows himself inside 'em.

Next Tom's fat legs they close invest,
And when they won't stretch tighter,
They're turned and shortened, washed and pressed,
And fixed on me, the writer.

Tramp—" Tell yer ledyship I ain't coming to 'er dance to-night."
Butler—" But you are not invited."
Tramp—" That's why I ain't comin'."

First Spectator—"That referee will be in hot water."
Second—" No, he'll be in the horse trough."

Boatman (to holiday merrymakers)—" I must ask you to pay in advance as the boat leaks."

# FUNLAND
## EVERYBODY'S PLAYMATE

PUZZLES, TRICKS, GAMES & MAGIC

★ BY ★ A.W. NUGENT THE WORLD'S LEADING PUZZLEMAKER

**S**HADE IN ALL THE LITTLE SECTIONS IN WHICH YOU SEE A DOT TO MAKE A PICTURE OF AN EX-PRESIDENT OF THE UNITED STATES.

**U**SE A SOFT PENCIL

**C**ONNECT ALL THE DOTS IN THEIR ORDER FROM DOT ONE TO DOT THIRTY-EIGHT TO COMPLETE THIS PICTURE

**C**UT OUT INDIANS TO COLOUR BEND AND STAND FIRST COLOUR THE TWO PICTURES WITH YOUR CRAYONS OR WATER COLOUR THEN CUT OUT THE TWO SKETCHES AROUND THEIR ENTIRE OUT-LINES. BEND THEM ON THE DOTTED LINES AS PER INSTRUCTIONS TO MAKE THEM STAND

BEND BACKWARD

BEND BACKWARD

**MARY HAD A LITTLE LAMB, ITS FLEECE WAS WHITE AS SNOW, AND EVERYWHERE THAT MARY WENT, THE LAMB WAS SURE TO GO**

**T**HESE SEVEN PIECES, WHEN CUT OUT, CAN BE PUT TOGETHER TO MAKE A PERFECT TRIANGLE – THAT IS WITH ALL OF ITS SIDES THE SAME LENGTH. CAN YOU DO IT?

**C**AN YOU DIVIDE THIS ENTIRE SQUARE INTO SIX SMALLER SQUARES OF TWO DIFFERENT SIZES?

**D**RAW YOUR LINES LIGHTLY, WITH A PENCIL, SO THEY MAY BE EASILY ERASED IF NECESSARY.

**B**END THE WIGWAM BACKWARD ON THE DOTTED LINE.

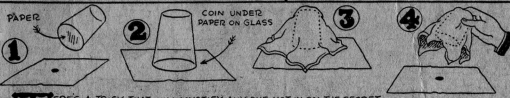

PAPER
COIN UNDER PAPER ON GLASS
① ② ③ ④

**H**ERE'S A TRICK THAT WILL MYSTIFY ANY ONE NOT IN ON THE SECRET. TAKE AN ORDINARY GLASS TUMBLER AND PASTE A PIECE OF PAPER OVER THE TOP OF IT, AS SHOWN IN FIG.1 THEN LAY A SHEET OF THE SAME PAPER (THIS IS IMPORTANT) ON A TABLE AND PLACE A COIN ON IT PUT THE TUMBLER OVER THE COIN; IT WILL APPEAR AS THOUGH THERE WERE NOTHING UNDER THE TUMBLER (FIG 2)
**S**HOW THE TUMBLER WITH NOTHING UNDER IT AND COVER IT WITH A HANDKERCHIEF, AS IN FIG. 3; RAISE THE GLASS AND THE HANDKERCHIEF AS SHOWN IN FIG 4, AND TO THE ASTONISHMENT OF ALL BEHOLDERS THE COIN APPEARS REPLACE THE TUMBLER AND REMOVE THE HANDKERCHIEF — PRESTO! THE COIN HAS VANISHED IF YOU ARE CAREFUL NOT TO LET ANY ONE SEE THE PAPER ON THE MOUTH OF THE GLASS YOU CAN REPEAT THIS TRICK ANY NUMBER OF TIMES.

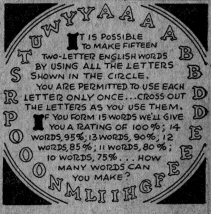

STUWYYAAAAB... (circle of letters)

**I**T IS POSSIBLE TO MAKE FIFTEEN TWO-LETTER ENGLISH WORDS BY USING ALL THE LETTERS SHOWN IN THE CIRCLE. YOU ARE PERMITTED TO USE EACH LETTER ONLY ONCE... CROSS OUT THE LETTERS AS YOU USE THEM. **I**F YOU FORM 15 WORDS WE'LL GIVE YOU A RATING OF 100%; 14 WORDS, 95%; 13 WORDS, 90%; 12 WORDS, 85%; 11 WORDS, 80%; 10 WORDS, 75%... HOW MANY WORDS CAN YOU MAKE?

**M**ISTRESS MARY, QUITE CONTRARY, HOW DOES YOUR GARDEN GROW? WITH COCKLE-SHELLS AND SILVER BELLS, AND PRETTY MAIDS ALL IN A ROW.

**C**OLOUR AND CUT OUT THE ENTIRE PICTURE. BEND THE SIDES BACKWARD TO MAKE HER STAND

**L**ITTLE ARTISTS' DRAWING LESSON. FIRST DRAW AN EGG, THEN ADD THE OTHER LINES

1 START

2

## SOLUTIONS TO LAST WEEK'S PUZZLES:

**L**ETTER CHANGING PUZZLE ANSWER KEY, KEG, LEG, LOG, HOG, DOG, DOE, HOE, TOE, TOP, MOP, COP, CUP, CAP.
THE EIGHT MISTAKES WERE:—
THE BULLDOG HAS ONE SHORT AND ONE LONG EAR, ONE LEG MISSING
THE ELEPHANTS TUSKS ARE TURNED WRONG WAY THE DUCK HAS A COCKSCOMB.
THE CAMEL HAS THREE HUMPS. THE COCK HAS ONLY TWO FRONT CLAWS ON EACH FOOT AND ONE SPUR IS MISSING; THE PIG HAS THE WRONG KIND OF TAIL

**F**ILL IN THE BLANK SPACES WITH THE FOLLOWING WORDS: SANG, SNAG, NAGS.

## FUNNY CORNER

# CHEEKY CONUNDRUMS

What part of London is like a lame man ?—Cripplegate (gait).

Why is a defeated team like wool ?—It's worsted.

What can you fill a barrel with yet make it lighter ?—Holes.

Which is easier to spell—fiddle-de-dee or fiddle-de-dum ?—The first, because it is spelt with more e's (ease).

Why can negroes be trusted with a secret ?—Because they always keep dark.

Where does charity begin ?—At C.

Why is a boy with a sore throat like a pony ?—He is a little horse (hoarse).

Why is a retired carpenter like a lecturer ?—He is an ex-planer.

What pudding makes the best cricketer ?—A good batter.

Why are gardeners better paid than other tradesmen ?—They have more celery (salary).

Why is a joke like a church bell ?—It is often tolled.

Why do carpenters believe there is no such thing as stone ?—Because they never saw it.

With what musical instrument would you catch a fish ?—Castanet.

Why is Ireland like a bottle ?—There's a Cork in it.

What is a Boy Scout's weakest point ?—His tenderfoot.

When is a boat like snow ?—When it's adrift.

Why is a pawnbroker like a silly boy ?—Because he will take anything in.

When is a candle in a passion ?—When it flares up.

What is the difference between the King and the moon ?—19s 11¾d. The King is a sovereign and the moon is a far-thing.

What colour does flogging make a boy ?—Yellow. (Yell oh !)

# STOP HERE FOR POETRY

## A TALE FOR T-TIME.

Ten thousand trippers
　Took twenty-three
Trains to take them
　To Trincomally.

They travelled towards
　The thickest tree.
They talked, they tittered,
　Then took their tea.

The tunes they trilled
　Together then,
The tales they told
　Till ten to ten.

Till tardy time
　Told them the tale,
To turn themselves
　To the townward trail.

## ANIMAL ARGUMENTS.

Said the lion, " Look here, fellows,
　I'm the main thing in this show."
Said the porcupine—" I won't have that,
　I have my points, you know."
The kangaroo got cocky—
　" I'm always on the jump."
" Oh, stop it," growled the camel,
　" You just give me the hump."

Said the polar bear, " I reckon
　I always take the bun."
The pelican remarked, " My bill
　Can hold about a ton."
Said the elephant, " My keeper
　At my food bill often quails."
The ortrich only gave a sniff,
　And said, " You can't eat nails."
" I take the prize," said the giraffe,
　" For being long and tall."
The hyena gave a chuckle,
　" I've the laugh upon you all."

## JUST GUFF.

It was a fine December morning,
In April last July.
The moon lay thick upon the ground,
The snow shone in the sky,
The flowers were sweetly singing,
The birds were in full bloom.
As I went to the basement
To clean the upstair room,
The time was Tuesday morning,
On Wednesday just at night,
I saw ten thousand miles away,
A house just out of sight.
The doors projected backwards,
The front was at the back.
It stood alone between two more,
And it was white-washed black.

# FUNNY THINGS TO MAKE

BILLY BONES

Cut body and limbs out of cardboard and fix with string

Cut Hector's feet out of cardboard and fix to figure with paper fastener

Stick matches into potato

THE SPUD-WHATISIT

HURRYING HECTOR

# What Does Your Name Mean

## Boys' Names.

**Adam**—Keen to succeed.
**Albert**—Born to be famous.
**Alexander**—Strong as a rock.
**Alfred**—Reliable, a good adviser.
**Algernon** — Pleasure - loving, selfish.
**Alister**—Difficult to please.
**Allan**—Even-tempered, sincere.
**Andrew**—Of noble thought.
**Archibald**—Bold observer.
**Arthur**—For a noble cause.
**Aubrey** — Fond of admiration.
**Bartholomew** — One of learning.
**Basil**—Willing to forgive.
**Benjamin**—Wants his own way.
**Bertram** — Changeable but lovable.
**Brian**—Strong-willed, fearless.
**Cecil**—A hard worker.
**Charles**—Manly.
**Clive**—Quick to decide.
**Colin**—One to be trusted.

## Girls' Names.

**Ada**—Contented, reliable.
**Agnes**—Strongminded, slow to anger.
**Aileen**—Bright and lovable.
**Alice**—Of great personality.
**Alison** — Successful, sympathetic.
**Amy**—Beloved, generous.
**Ann, Anna or Annie**—Gracious, most observant.
**Anette**—Faithful and true.
**Audrey**—Capable of fame.
**Avril**—Sunny-natured and care-free.
**Barbara**—Shy and retiring.
**Beatrice**—Fond of sharing happiness.
**Bessie**—Home - loving, good-tempered.
**Brenda**—Of noble descent.
**Bridget**—Strong in character.
**Catherine**—Forgiving.
**Clara**—Born to be famous.

# PA "NOSE" WHAT TO DO

THAT'S A MISERABLE LIGHT!

THIS CANDLE WILL DO THE TRICK!

AH! THIS IS BETTER!

# THE TRAMP'S BEDROOM

THE GRASS IS TOO WET TO HAVE A NAP ON!

AH! THIS OLD GAMP GIVES ME AN IDEA!

HOW'S THAT?

# A PLEASANT SATURDAY AFTERNOON IN AUCHENTOGLE

If you want to see REAL red-blooded football come to the Paradise Road Football Ground up in Auchentogle. Admission by season ticket, 4d cash, or 3 jam jars.

Here's the great semi-final between the Dubbin Alley Celtic and the Whigmaleerie Rangers in the Juvenile Alliance Cup. (Juvenile means players up to and including the age of 50.) Despite other attractions in the district, such as a Jumble Sale, an Oddfellows' Procession, and a couple of First Division games, there was a huge crowd, and the takings amounted to 4/11, a bad shilling, and 80 jam jars.

The grand stands (one tree and one notice board) were well patronised. The police had a busy time. Look at P.C. Flannelfeet chasing the dog fancier who set his bull pup on the linesman for a free meal, while P.C. Spudd got into an argument with the crowd and missed half the game. The game was a binder. Rangers in stripes managed to slip 13 men on to the field, then raised a row because the Celtic, in white, were playing with 14. Sheer jealousy.

One of the best goals was the result of scientific play. While the Celts were mobbing Referee M'Leerie to give a penalty, Rangers raided their goal. Slasher Jock, the outside-right, held the Celts' goalie back. Toughy Magee, the inside-left squashed the Celtic right-half against the goalpost, while the centre-forward bust the net with a shot that bust the photographer from the Sporting Special.

But were the Celts downhearted? Nae fears. Just look at the Rangers' skipper, Big Alec, being carried off after what they did to him. The funeral is on Tuesday. They dismembered the man with the whistle, and a fervid supporter scored a bull's eye with one cat, shop soiled and mostly dead, on the helmet of S— Macdoodle.

After thi[s] more a[...] and a [...] had by [...] break [...]

The tales from Auchentogle starred Jock McDade and featured in The Sunday Post Fun section alongside Oor Wullie and the Broons. These tales continued until after the War when poor Jock McDade was parked, but Oor Wullie and The Broons marched on.

Printed and Published in Great Britain by D. C. Thomson & Co., Ltd., 144 [...] anan Street, N., Glasgow.

The artist behind Oor Wullie and The Broons was Dudley D. Watkins, born in Manchester in 1907. His family moved to Nottingham where he was brought up. His artistic talent was noticed early and by the age of ten was declared an artistic genius. At seventeen he entered Glasgow School of Art and within a year was offered a six month trial period by D.C.Thomson in Dundee . Six months turned into forty four years. His output was prolific, varied and innovative. This illustration of Dudley D. Watkins was painted by staff artist, David Gudgeon, and shows the man at his easel in his studio.

# They Had A Grand Day At The Zoo;
## But The Animals Came In Two By Two.

# When To The Polish They Got Doon,
# They Called Paw Robinson-Crusoe Broon.

## Wullie Fancied Himself Asleep In The Deep.
## There's Deep-Seated Reasons Why He Canna Sleep.

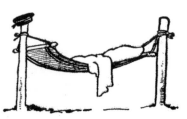

# When Up To London The Family Went,
# The Broons Fair Made Their Presence Kent.

## When Wullie Visited Aunt Mabel
## He Was Just As Good As He Was Able.

# THE BRAW BROONS

(To the tune " WEEL MAY THE KEEL ROW.")

MAW BROON'S a braw Broon
A nae-bother-at-a' Broon.
It's really her that ca's the tune
For the family.

Paw Broon's a sma' Broon,
The daddy-o'-them-a' Broon.
Nothing ever gets him doon
Except his family!

Maggie Broon's anither Broon,
A lassie Broon, a classy Broon.
She mak's the lads swoon,
But no her family.

Daphne Broon's the saft Broon,
The daft Broon, the chaffed Broon,
You'll be laughin' at her soon
And at her family.

Hen Broon's the lang Broon,
The tallest o' the gang Broon.
The only lad that looks doon
At his family.

Joe Broon's a tough Broon,
A rough Broon, a bluff Broon.
Ready aye tae gie a tune
Tae please the family.

The twins, tae, are ca'ed Broon,
Double Broon, trouble Broon!
Something o' a mixed boon—
Tae the family.

Horace is the swotty Broon,
The spotty Broon, the potty Broon.
The never, never naughty Broon
O' the family.

Gran'paw Broon's a fine Broon,
A couthy auld-lang-syne Broon.
He'll be ninety-nine soon!
What a family!

The Bairn Broon's the wee Broon,
The latest yin tae be Broon.
The aipple-o'-Paw's-e'e Broon,
An' that's the family!

# Granpaw Is Eighty-Eight Years Young;
## They'll Hae Him Shot, If He's No' Hung.

# BEES, BUGS, MIDGIES, FORKIES AND CREEPY CRAWLIES—BEWARE!

Mrs Buggs is Auchentogle's kind old lady. She knits socks for South Sea Islanders and buys ice-cream barrows for Eskimos, and all that sort of thing.

Last week she offered a pound of peppermints to the boy who had the best collection of local insect life by Saturday.

All the lads knew about insects was that butterflies flutter by and dragon-flies drink flagons dry. But that didn't stop them from forming an Insect-Collectors' Club.

Ham nets, fishing nets, hair nets, and even tennis rackets were used, but even then the net results were poor. Half a dozen gnats (pronounced "midgies"), a few bees, and enough wasps to cover a threepeny were captured.

Jock Short and Willie Short rigged up a treacle trap for bees. They spread treacle pieces to draw out the insects, while Alick Short lay behind a bush (it was an am-bush) ready to swoop down on them. But by the time the bees got there, the cupboard was bare. Jock

and Willie had eaten all the bait themselves!

With his smart invention of the Fly Paper on the End of a Stick, Dosey Tamson chased a long-winded butterfly half a mile, then stepped into a burn. It took him up to the ankles. But he went in head first!

The crows are thinking of hiring Johnny Magee as a beater. Every butterfly he missed they just had to snap up. That would be easier for them than getting up at six o'clock in the morning to catch the early worm. Johnny was so annoyed at missing the butterflies that he blamed his pal.

"You're aye hurting my heel with your chin!" he growled at Chick Forbes.

"There's nothing to sting me here!" said Jock M'Dade with a sigh of relief as he sat down. But he sat down in a bed of nettles.

Nobody won the prize. By Saturday night Mrs Buggs had eaten all the peppermints.

*Printed and Published in Great Britain by D. C. Thomson & Co., Ltd., 144 Port Dundas Road, Buchanan Street, N., Glasgow.*

## If You Would Not Be " On The Rocks,"
## Don't Save In The Bairn's Money-Box.

# The Broons Tried Jam To Make One Day.
## Now They're A "Stuck-Up" Family!

SUPPLEMENT TO THE SUNDAY POST, SEPTEMBER 27, 1936.

## Poor Paw! He's Gettin' Fairly Roastit;
## His Coupon Was Richt.    But He Didna Post It.

SUPPLEMENT TO THE SUNDAY POST, OCTOBER 18, 1936.

# The Broons Got A Pet, But Regret It.

## Ye See They've Nae Place Tae Pet It!

# Braw Fun On The Railway

"There's a big red injin in the station," roared Jock M'Dade, rushing up into the middle of his gang and giving Eck Wilson a smack in the ear for nothing.

"Does he ha'e feathers in his hair an' a lot o' scalps hanging roond his wigwam?" gasped wee Ecky Drumtochty.

"It's no' that kind of an injin," replied Jock. "It's a railway injin wi' wheels on. Dod Patterson's faither drove it in the day an' now he's awa' for his dinner. An' I've given wee Dod twa granny-sookers an' a look at ma white mice tae get him tae tak' us doon an' see his faither's injin. Come on!"

When the lads arrived at the station, they went wild with excitement. You see, Auchentogle stands on the old Bummieshanter-to-Inverness line, and the folk think it's a grand joke to call the engines "slowcomotives." but this engine wasn't one of the usual old wheezy kind. Oh no! Jings, it even had a name, "The Prince of Peerieblaw," printed on its side.

In a jiffy, you couldn't see that engine for the youth of Auchentogle swarming on it.

Sammy Samson booked his seat on a queer wee hump on the boiler, But that was the steam whistle, and, when Jock M'Dade pulled a cord and blew it, the steam made Sammy jump so fast that his shadow was half a minute in catching him up.

Then Jock turned and asked wee Ecky Drumtochty why he was crying. Ecky pointed to a lever he'd been twiddling.

"I've turned it till that thing says 'Explosion Point,'" Ecky sobbed. "An' the injin hasna' exploded at a'."

"The very dab," cried Jim Short, when he found the boiler was full of braw boiling water. His mother takes in washing and Jim helped her by carting a load of dirty clothes down to the station and washing them. It's a pity the water was so hot. The white things came out coloured and the coloured things came out white.

Chick Forbes oiled the wheels with glue, and Sandy M'Nab toasted herring at the funnel till he was as brown as a smokie.

But the funniest thing was Joe M'Ara carrying home the engine wheels for his wee brother's Meccano.

Fortunately, Jock M'Dade was playing "Hielan' Laddie" on the steam whistle, and that brought Mr Patterson down in time to stop Joe taking the boiler.

Just as Jock M'Dade had fun on the railway, trains were a source of fun and adventure for children, and a lot of adults. Weekend trips were often by train, as were longer journeys. Steam trains have always held a fascination for boys who would hang over the parapet of a bridge to get engulfed by smoke, not to mention sparks. This train was photographed from the pedestrian bridge at Magdalen Green Station, Dundee. Note the sheep grazing on the Magdalen Green, something that continued every year until the mid 1960s.

# THE SUNDAY POST FUN SECTION
## 'OOR WULLIE'

SUPPLEMENT TO THE SUNDAY POST.
NOVEMBER 29, 1936.

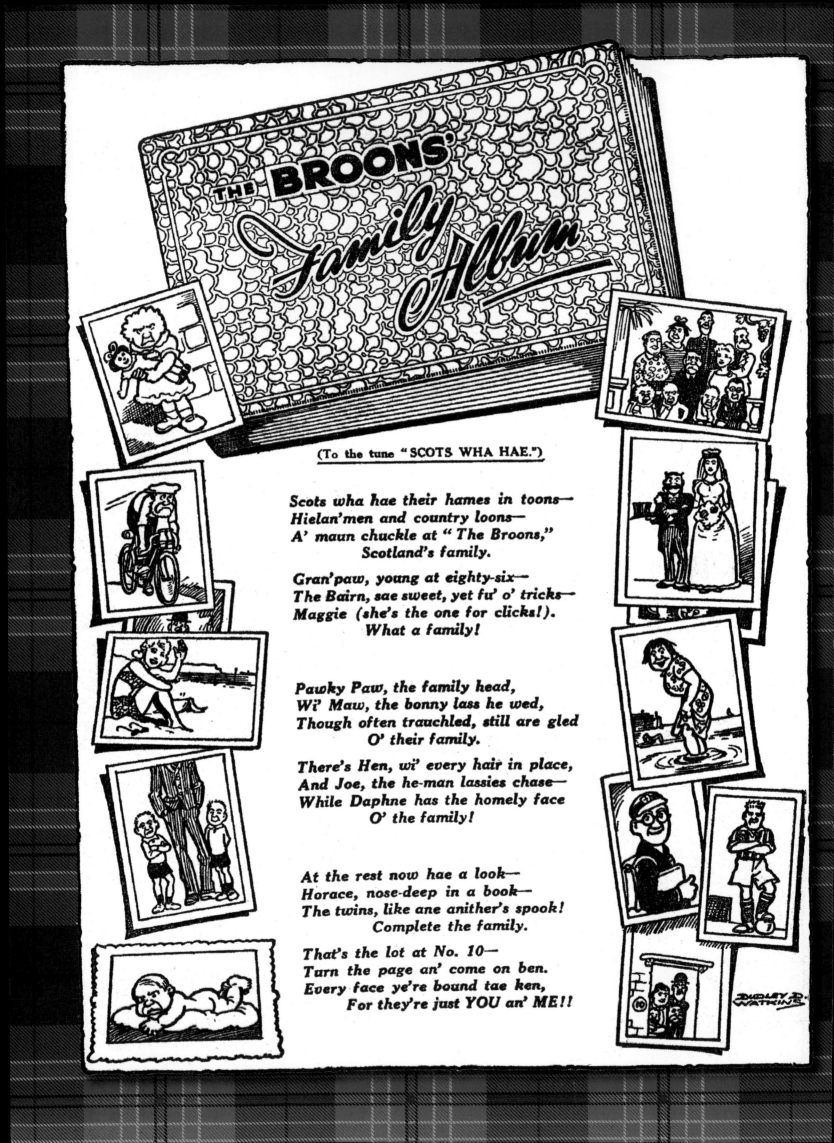

# OOR WULLIE

*Wha keeps his mother in a steer ?*
*Wha nearly drives his father queer ?*
*Wha throws the whole town oot o' gear ?*
  *—Oor Wullie !*
*Wha has the teacher on a string ?*
*Wha keeps the bobby wondering ?*
*Wha pets his feet in everything ?*
  *—Oor Wullie !*

*Wha is't, as soon's the day's begun,*
*Is thinking how he'll hae some fun,*
*And starts whene'er his breakfast's done ?*
  *—Oor Wullie !*
*Wha ilka day has some ploy new,*
*And shares them a' wi me and you ?*
*Wha dreams o' jokin' a' nicht through ?*
  *—Oor Wullie*

*Wha sits upon his wee zinc pail*
*And thinks oot schemes that canna fail ?*
*—It puzzles me he's no in jail—*
  *—Oor Wullie !*
*Wha is't, whate'er the complication,*
*On each and every occasion*
*Has aye some handy explanation ?*
  *—Oor Wullie !*

*Wha is't that in his dungarees*
*Sits thinking oot some brand-new wheeze*
*That sets fowk shaking at the knees ?*
  *—Oor Wullie !*
*Wha is't, despite oor toil and trouble,*
*Wi' lauchin' gars us bend near double,*
*And maks us fair wi' pleasure bubble ?*
  *—Oor Wullie !*

# The Broons Stage An " At Home."
## That Isn't On The Programme.

SUPPLEMENT TO THE SUNDAY POST, DECEMBER 6, 1956.

# THE SUNDAY POST FUN SECTION

## 'OOR WULLIE'

## They Have A Proverb In The Toon—
### "Save's Frae The Luck O' Poor Paw Broon!"

## Now Wullie Has One Golden Rule—
## "A Doctor's Leg Ye Canna Pull!"

## *The Broons Wish You All*
## *As Merry A Christmas As They Got !*

## Wullie Managed To Mind The Bairn,
## But In Mindin' The Rest He Wasna Spairin'.

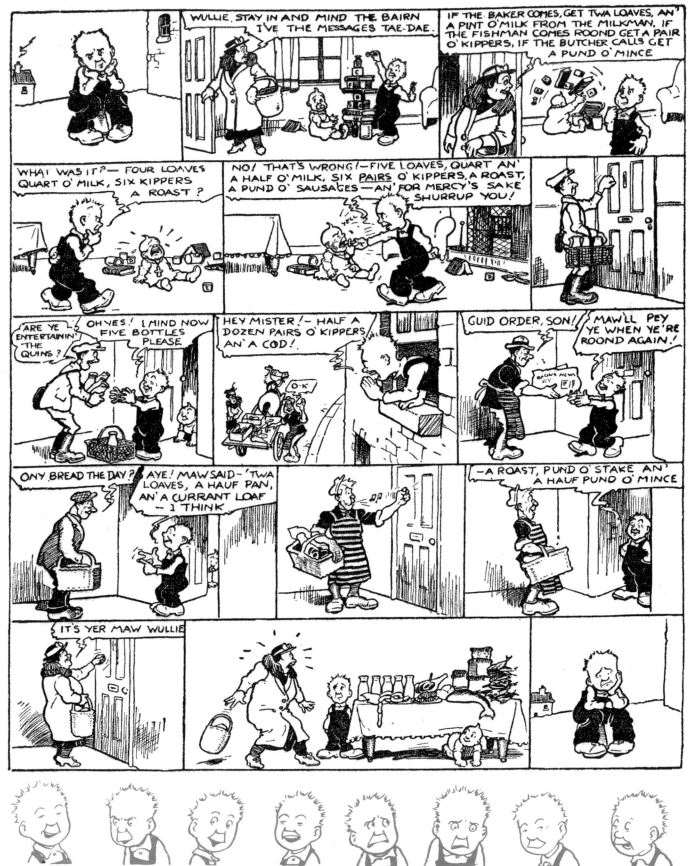

# JOCK M'DADE THE WASHER-WIFE!

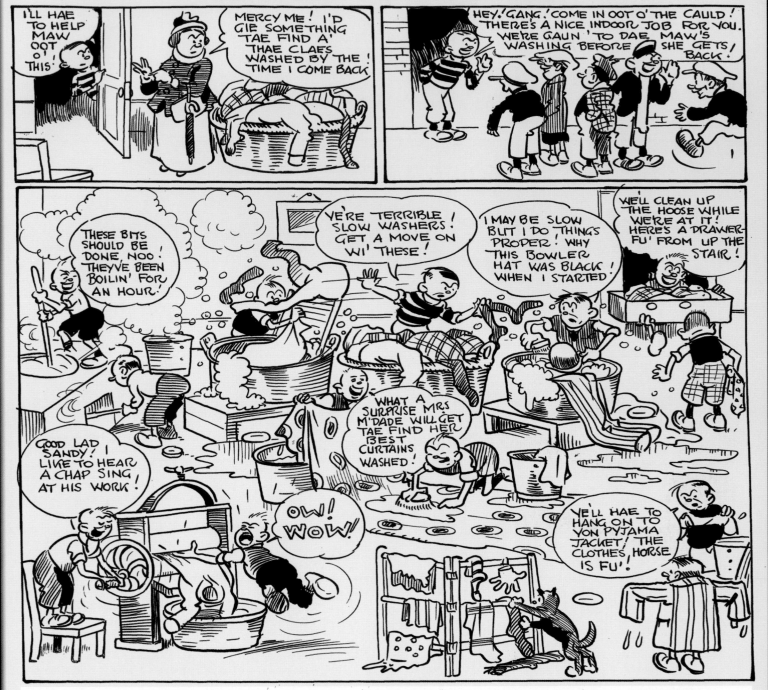

"It's a sair fecht," sighed Mrs M'Dade. "The morn's washing day and Tam's dungarees are so thick with grease that they could almost walk doon to the wash-hoose by themsel's. Twa pair o' thick blankets, tae! And all these dirty hankies – you'd think they cleaned their boots with them!"

But there was a good fairy with freckles and a striped jersey just around the corner. It was Jock M'Dade! As soon as the house stopped shaking, he knew his mother was safe downstairs, and he called in his gang to do the washing.

You should have seen the lads tear into the job. Knee-deep in soap-suds and up to the eyebrows in steam, they tubbed and scrubbed and rubbed, and they weren't too pernickety as long as they got results.

Spud Wilson laid a pair of curtains from the parlour on the floor. He swept them down with a besom first, and then went over them with a scrubbing brush until their red roses had faded into white lilies.

At the mangle, Eck Short was playing a hardy game, busting up buttons and splitting down seams. "Stop the dancing and get on with the work", he snapped to Sandy M'Nab, his assistant.

"Dancing be hanged!" howled Sandy. "Ah'm no' dancing. My fingers are caught in the rollers!"

The boiler was in command of Dosey Tamson, and Dosey's one of those cocky lads who would try and teach a herring to swim. He didn't know much about boiling clothes, but he'd seen his mother boiling soup. So Dosey boiled the clothes for a couple of hours, and it's a wonder he didn't pepper and salt them.

"Look at this, Jock" he called proudly, holding up one of Mr M'Dade's shirts. 'It's shrunk a bit, but it's as white as snow!"

"Aye," groaned Jock. "And that's faither's best broon shirt, you gomeril. Now you'd better try and boil Pa doon to a dwarf to get into it."

And when Mrs M'Dade came home she looked sadly at the remains, then sent Jock for the rag-man.

"And you'd better buy a new belt on the way home," she called after him. "Your father's lost his old one and he'll be needing another."

## *Keep The Home Fires Burning!*
## *But The Kippers Needed Turning.*

## Though The Box Of Tricks Produced Loud Squeals,
## Wull's Safer Wi' His Box On Wheels.

# The Loudest, Strongest Best Loud-Speaker
# Beside The Broons Is Just A Squeaker.

# Wullie Doesna Think It's Fair
# To Have No Fare When The Weather's No' Fair.

## *Polishing Day At The Broons'—*
## *And Paw Is Nearly Polished Off!*

# Poor Wullie's Fortune-Telling Try-On

## Was Not A Thing He Could Rely On.

# A Burglar At The Broons!
## Send For The " Polis "!

## If To Be Wull's Pal's Your Intention
## A Vacuum-Cleaner Dinna Mention.

# Paw Gets Wound-Up,
## And Ma Gets Wind-up.

# MEET THE BROONS!

They live in Glebe Street, Number Ten,
But dinna knock—juist haud richt
  ben ;
For a' the fowk for miles roond ken
    The Broons !
Fower bairns, three weemen an' fower
  men.
    The Broons !

Weel, first there's Maw, and she's a'
  richt!
She works at hame frae morn tae
  nicht.
But while she toils her he'rt is licht.
    Maw Broon!
There's juist ae family in her sicht—
    The Broons!

Ilk mornin' o' his married days
Paw Broon has donned his working
  claes,
An' tae the shipyard turned his taes.
    Paw Broon!
That's whaur he gets bawbees tae raise
    The Broons!

Now meet the lads! Well, first there's
  Hen,
Who is so " awf'lly spick and spen!"
He's quite "pan-loaf," while Joe is
  " plenn."
    Thae Broons!
But, toff and tough, they're real he-
  men—
    Thae Broons!

There's Horace next. He looks a Jess!
A lad o' pairts, though, nane the less.
And then twin laddies cam' tae bless
    The Broons!
A pair o' rogues aye in a mess—
    Thae Broons!

Now Daphne's got the kind o' face
Ca'd "sonsy "—but that's nae dis-
  grace,
For Daphne's he'rt's in the richt place.
    A Broon!
Forbye, there's Maggie's looks tae
  grace
    The Broons!

An' then the Bairn we'll no' forget.
O' a' the family she's the pet.
An' Grandpaw, I've no' mentioned yet.
    A Broon!
That auld lad's ploys can whiles upset
    The Broons!

And so ye've met them yin by yin,
A happy bunch through thick and thin.
Blest in their hearts if no' wi' tin,
    The Broons!
For they're juist YOU and a' YOUR
  kin—
    The Broons!

PAW BROON    MAW BROON    MAGGIE BROON    HEN BROON    DAPHNE BROON    JOE BROON    HORACE BROON    THE BROON TWINS    THE BROON BAIRN    GRAN' PAW BROON

# Paw Whistles To Wull, When He Wants A Lark,
## The Tune 'I'm Afraid To Go Home In The Dark.'

# Everyone Has Fish and Chips.

## But Paw Has To Fish Out The Dibs!

## This Story Tells How Bully Bates
## Took On A Lot When He Took Wull's Skates.

## Paw Broon Can't Believe His Eyes,
## When Joe Walks In With The "Prize."

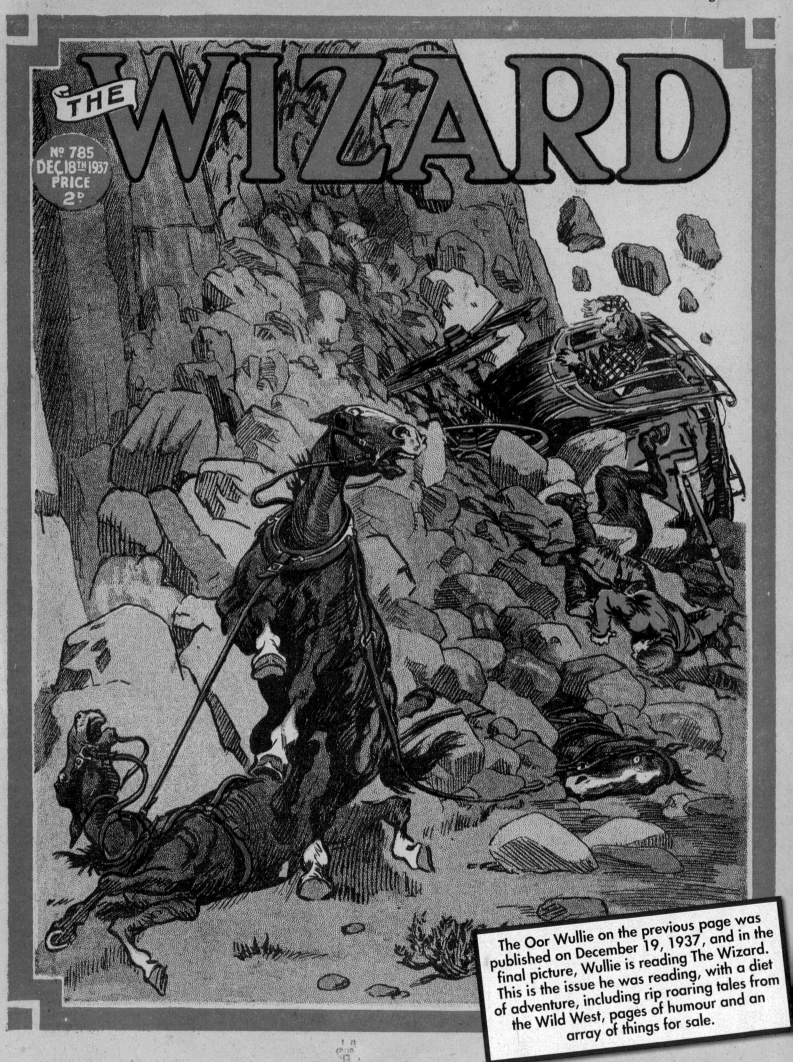

STORIES WITH A BIG THRILL

"The Seven Plagues From Silent Swamp"
"The Terror Strikes On Moonless Nights"

THE WIZARD

Nº 785
DEC 18TH 1937
PRICE
2D

The Oor Wullie on the previous page was published on December 19, 1937, and in the final picture, Wullie is reading The Wizard. This is the issue he was reading, with a diet of adventure, including rip roaring tales from the Wild West, pages of humour and an array of things for sale.

# PHANTOM CHAMPION OF THE WEST

## Four Rawhide Double-Crossers

BURSTS of laughter came from a private room in the Silver Dollar Saloon, which was situated in the main street of Virginia City, Nevada. Four hard-faced rodeo riders Quirt Ruddock, Shooter Skaith, Loop Durgan, and Rapid Rickson, sat round a table in the back room of the saloon, hooting with laughter as they studied a letter which Quirt Ruddock had received from Jake Transom, owner of a travelling circus.

"Haw! Haw! Haw!" guffawed Quirt Ruddock, the buck-jumping expert. "This guy's asking us to take the place of Trig M'Fee in his circus show. Well, if that don't beat the band!"

"You've said it," leered Loop Durgan, who specialised in roping events. "And offering us real money for doing it. Anyway, it's our duty to take Trig M'Fee's place. That was what we got rid of him for, wasn't it?"

"You bet it was," grinned Shooter Skaith, hitching up his fancy, pearl-handled guns. "Two hundred dollars for showing ourselves off in a circus isn't to be sneezed at."

Ruddock banged his fist down on the table. "But we ain't going to take the job," he sneered.

His companions gaped at him.

"Refuse to take an easy job worth two hundred dollars?" gulped Rapid Rickson.

"Sure! We can make a pile of money if we make use of this guy's offer in another way."

As his companions still looked blank, Ruddock slowly read over Jake Transom's letter on the table in front of him. In the letter the circus owner explained how he had recently heard of the tragic death of Trig M'Fee, and how this had seriously upset his arrangements.

It appeared that Jake and Trig M'Fee, the famous rodeo champion, had been very good friends. As a special favour, Trig had agreed to join the circus for a special performance in the big middle-western town of Kentonville, one of Jake's most important visits for his circus.

He had shrewdly decided that Kentonville lay too far east for its people to have had much chance of seeing real rodeo events, and that a first-class Wild West exhibition was certain to draw a bumper crowd to the circus.

Overjoyed, the circus owner had lost no time before posting big advance bills over the town promising the Middle-Westerners a real treat, and advertising the rodeo show as his star attraction. Then, like a bombshell, had come the tragic news of Trig M'Fee's terrible death amid the blazing ruins of Rawhide jail.

The circus owner had read a full account of the story of how Trig M'Fee had been accused of shooting a stagecoach driver in cold blood, and arrested. That same night a lynching mob had stormed the jail and burned it to the ground. A metal belt-buckle was all that had been found among the ashes. Trig M'Fee had perished in the flames!

The circus owner's letter concluded by pointing out how Trig M'Fee's death had spoiled his Kentonville arrangements. He had promised the townsfolk a star exhibition of rodeo events. Failure to carry out his promise would do his circus a great deal of harm in the town. That was why he was so keen to get the gang of rodeo riders to come along to take Trig's place.

**You'll read here about the town that gets rid of crooks by shaving pieces of wood!**

"You poor saps," jeered Ruddock, as he flicked the letter with his fingers. "Can't you see how this circus guy has played right into our hands?"

"How?" demanded his hard-faced pals.

"By letting us know how keen the Kentonville folks will be to see a real Western show! If Jake Transom can afford to pay us two hundred dollars to bring the crowd into his circus, he's going to make a lot more for himself, ain't he? So why should we make money for him when we can give our own show and collect all the profits for ourselves!"

"Give our own show?" echoed the three other rodeo riders, as Ruddock's dazzling idea dawned upon them.

"Sure!" chuckled Ruddock. "There's a big baseball ground outside Kentonville. We can hire it for next to nothing at this time of year. It's a great place for giving a rodeo display. We've only to give our show on the same day as the circus to rope in Transom's big crowd. That way, we'll make thousands of dollars instead of two hundred."

"Then you ain't going to tell him that we're putting on our own show?"

"You bet we ain't!" leered Ruddock. "We'll just tell him that we'll be along to Kentonville on circus day. He'll carry on advertising our Western display as his star attraction. He'll get the shock of his life when he finds he's advertised an opposition show, but he won't be able to do anything to stop us!"

Again and again the back room of the saloon echoed with the gang's howls of laughter as they completed their plans for making a fool of Trig M'Fee's friend. The thing was to keep Jake Transom hanging on as long as possible. So long as no outsider got to hear of their plot, they were certain that things couldn't go wrong this time.

Meanwhile, to cover their tracks, they would keep clear of Kentonville. They could easily appoint an agent to hire the baseball ground and make other preliminary arrangements through the post.

Even the mysterious masked enemy, who had foiled their efforts to win rodeo prizes since Trig M'Fee's death, couldn't interfere with their crafty plot if he knew nothing about it!

Rapid Rickson had no further doubts that he and his pals were at last due to make plenty money out of getting rid of Trig M'Fee.

"It's a great stunt, Quirt," he chuckled, admiringly. "Everything's made to measure and nothing can stop us from raking in a pile of dollars."

"You've said it!" chorused the others.

Rising to their feet, they slapped Ruddock on the back. Then, chuckling and grinning all over their faces, they stamped away out of the saloon to send a misleading telegram to Jake Transom.

Then a strange thing happened in the room they had just left. The delighted grins would have vanished from their brutal faces had they happened to look back. A masked figure in black hat, shirt, and neckerchief, appeared from where he had been standing motionless behind the long curtains that covered the window recess.

"So that's their game, is it?" muttered the masked man grimly. "To double-cross old Jake. I'll have to see what I can do about it!"

The plotters would have been still more astounded had they seen the grim, fire-scarred face under the mask. It would have told them that Trig M'Fee, their great rival in rodeo events, had not perished amid the blazing ruins of Rawhide jail after all!

## The Phantom's Free-for-All

ALTHOUGH Trig had escaped the vengeance of the Rawhide lynching mob, it was still impossible for him to resume his ordinary life. He was still unable to prove his innocence of the terrible crime for which he had been arrested.

Until he could do so, he must remain a nameless outlaw. He knew that Ruddock and his pals, his bitter rivals in rodeo events, had framed him and had him thrown into jail to get him out of the way. Meanwhile, however, he could only do his best to make sure that they shouldn't profit by his supposed death.

A grim smile twisted his lips as he thought of the many times he had baulked them in his masked disguise as the mysterious Phantom Campion.

A week later, he rode towards Kentonville astride his big black horse. He now wore the dress of a wandering cowboy. So far east there was small danger of anyone recognising him as the famous Western rodeo star who was supposed to be dead.

He reined in outside the baseball ground on the outskirts of the town. The fence round the ground was plastered with new bills. They announced—

THE ONLY WESTERN SHOW IN KENTONVILLE!
GREAT RODEO DISPLAY BY STAR RIDERS.
Roll Up On Wednesday At 2 p.m.
Admission—1 Dollar.

Jake Transom's bills announced that the circus was due to open an hour later on the same day.

"The dirty dogs," breathed Trig. "Ruddock and his pals think that they've got everything cut and dried to collar the circus crowd!"

To-day was Monday. That meant that Trig had the following day to spike the gang's guns. He noticed a number of workmen preparing the ground for the display. A gleam in his eye, he rode over to their foreman.

"I've come on in advance of the riders who are giving this show," he drawled. "I'm thinking about giving a special show to-morrow to work up local interest. How does that fit in with your arrangements?"

"We can have everything ready to-morrow morning," replied the foreman in charge. "We've only to bring the steers for the hog-tying and bull-dogging up from the railway. But we've been paid for only one show. It'll cost you another twenty dollars, cash down as before, for the extra work."

Trig was delighted to hear that the workmen had been paid in advance for their work. That suited him down to the ground. He didn't want honest men to suffer because of Ruddock and his pals.

"Okay," he grinned, stripping a twenty-dollar note from the bulky wad of prize-money he had won as the Phantom Champion. "It's well worth it. Have everything fixed up for two o'clock to-morrow."

Delighted with the success of his opening move to spoil Ruddock's plans, he rode on towards the town.

"It's a good beginning, hoss," he chuckled, patting his big black's glossy neck. "And now——"

He stopped in amazement at an extraordinary sight. A big crowd had suddenly appeared from the streets of Kentonville. They were hustling a dishevelled, flashily-dressed man in front of them. But it was the way they were forcing their victim to keep him moving that was so strange.

Not a man of the crowd said a word. But every one of them carried a pocket-knife and a bit of stick. Whenever their victim tried to stop, they crowded round him and steadily whittled shavings from their sticks all over his flashy clothes!

It certainly got on their victim's nerves. With a hoarse cry he tried to shake himself clear. The crowd gave him no rest, however. Whittling away at their sticks like mad they kept on hustling him down the road to the railway station.

"What's the idea?" Trig asked an old fellow in the rear of the crowd.

"Just an old Kentonville custom," was the chuckling reply. "That's how we get rid of crooked gamblers and such-like polecats. Kentonville has no use for dirty dogs, so we whittle them out of town!"

An admiring gleam came into Trig's eyes.

"Gosh!" he murmured thoughtfully. "Whittle them out of town—that's a great idea!"

Grinning at Kentonville's queer way of getting rid of undesirables, Trig rode into the town. In Main Street he spotted the office of the local agent who sold tickets in advance.

One side was marked "Book Here For Transom's Circus." The other window had the announcement "Book here For Rodeo Display." There was a queue of eager buyers at the second window, but nobody was buying circus tickets.

"I'll have to put that right," Trig muttered grimly.

And late that night a mysterious masked figure moved round all the hoardings in the town. Armed with a brush and pot of red paint, he silently made an addition in glaring letters right across the Rawhide rodeo riders' bills.

"This should make the Kentonville folks sit up and take notice," he chuckled.

The people of Kentonville didn't like crooks and double-crossers—and they had a strange way of showing their dislike.

Next morning, the glaring red addition scrawled across the bills caused a sensation in the town. It was what many people dream about, but seldom see—a straightforward offer of something for nothing.

SPECIAL ADVANCE SHOW TO-DAY
ADMISSION FREE!

said the addition to the posters, and it certainly seemed too good to be true.

"Admission free!" exclaimed the people of Kentonville. "There must be a catch somewhere. It's either a hoax, or the show won't be worth watching!"

Despite their doubts, however, a huge crowd turned out at the baseball ground at two o'clock. Their doubts began to disappear when they saw the gates wide open and the ground all prepared for a full display of rodeo events.

Eagerly they rushed forward to get good places. When the ground was absolutely crowded out, they waited tensely for the free show. They hadn't long to wait for the excitement to begin. A gasp of amazement went up as the masked figure of the Phantom Champion suddenly appeared astride his big black horse.

At full gallop he raced round and round the ground, yipping and waving his black hat in thrilling cowboy style.

"What's the idea of the mask get-up?" men began to ask their neighbours.

"It's only an advertising stunt to make us wonder!" grinned the knowing ones among the crowd.

The people of Kentonville would have got the shocks of their lives had they known that the masked rider was really a much-wanted outlaw!

The Phantom reined his big horse back on its haunches. Cupping his hands round his mouth, he began to address the rows and rows of gaping spectators in a loud, clear voice.

"You're wondering why this show is free," he cried. "I'll tell you. The display of rodeo events I am about to give should really be part of Transom's Circus.

"But there's a gang of impostors out to do the dirty on Jake Transom. They claim to be star riders, but they're only a bunch of second-raters. I'll prove that every Western championship they claim to hold is really held by me.

"Their game is to follow Transom's Circus to get a good crowd. They then swindle the spectators out of hard-earned dollars with a second-rate display. That's why I'm here a day in advance to show them up with a real championship display. But I'll leave you to judge that for yourselves when you've seen the display."

The Phantom swept off his black hat.

"Thanking you one and all for the time being," he said, as he rose high in the stirrups.

And before the gaping spectators got their breaths back properly, the display started in thrilling fashion. A big steer, bellowing, and tossing its horns, suddenly rushed from one of the enclosures. For the moment the

# When twenty thousand people cheered a "wanted" man.

spectators couldn't decide whether it had been released intentionally or had broken loose.

It seemed that the bellowing brute had escaped and was running wild. The mysterious masked rider seemed frozen to his saddle as the steer thundered straight at him. Then, at the last moment, the big horse reared up on its hind legs.

"Ah-h-h!" A long-drawn gasp of relief went up as the tossing horns raised the rider's leg by inches. Quicker than the eye could follow a lasso snaked out as the enraged brute thundered past. Its loud hoofs thudded down, and the expertly thrown loop—

In a twinkling it was thrown on its side, and the Phantom Champion was hurtling down from the saddle on top of it. Then he sprang from his feet leaving the bellowing steer helpless, its boots expertly tied together with "pigging string."

It was a dazzling exhibition of the art of hog-tying. The Kentonville folks woke the echoes with their amazed cheers.

And so to think we're seeing it all for nothing," they gasped.

They nearly cheered their heads off when the Phantom's display came to an end.

"Are you satisfied that I'm no impostor?" he asked.

"You bet we are!" they yelled.

"Well," boomed the Phantom, "I think you Kentonville folks know how to deal with any crooks and twisters who come into your town!"

One small difficulty remained to be cleared up. These people among the crowd who had bought their tickets in advance for the Rawhide rodeo riders show wanted to know what they should do about it.

"After seeing your great show for nothing," they pointed out, "we won't want to use the tickets for a second-rate show."

"Don't worry," chuckled the Phantom, or show?"

"I've fixed that up with the ticket agent. Go along to his office, and I think you'll be quite satisfied!"

## Kentonville Vengeance!

QUIRT RUDDOCK and his pals and Jake Transom's Circus, arrived in Kentonville next day. Jake's pitch was on the opposite side of the town from the baseball ground, and the double-crossing rodeo riders thought it wise to keep out of his way.

"Guess he'll feel like a bear with a sore head when he sees what we've sprung on him!" chuckled Ruddock.

his hands strayed under the counter.

"So you're the Star Rodeo Riders'!"

"Yes. And we've come to collect our money right now."

"Then you'll have to collect it somewhere else," snapped the agent. "I'm a respectable business man, I am. You won't get me swindling my customers. All the money for your rotten tickets has been returned or exchanged for seats in Transom's Circus!"

The gang nearly dropped. Then, with enraged howls, their hands darted for their gun-butts. But the little agent was too quick for them. Like magic his hands appeared from under the counter, with a double-barrelled shot-gun.

"This is loaded up with buckshot!" he snapped. "One wrong move and I'll blow the lot of you into the middle of next week!"

With his left hand he jerked up the shutter of his pay-box.

"Come on, boys," he cried. "The swindlers the masked rider warned us about are in here trying to hold me up."

That did it. Instantly the smarting rodeo riders were surrounded by the crowd rushing into the office. Their guns were yanked from their holsters and the cartridges spilled on the floor.

Raving and bellowing, Ruddock and his pals were hustled into the street to become the victims of Kentonville's own strange method of getting rid of undesirables.

Everybody started to whittle their sticks like mad, remorselessly pressing closer and closer and showering their shavings over the flashy Western finery of the rodeo riders.

Nobody took the slightest notice of the ravings about the masked rider being the figure of the Phantom Champion, a badly-wanted outlaw. When the citizens of Kentonville made up their minds to whittle undesirables out of town they had no time for anything else.

At last, dishevelled, wild-eyed, and smothered in shavings, the rodeo riders were hustled right out to the baseball ground. There they were only too glad to throw themselves on their horses and disappear in a cloud of dust. Nothing was more certain than that they would never dare to show their faces in Kentonville again.

"That's that!" roared the crowd delightedly. "Now we'll all get back to the circus!"

As they streamed back to give Jake Transom's bumper audience, the masked figure of the Phantom Champion put away his powerful field-glasses. Astride his big black horse he had watched the whole scene from a nearby hilltop.

"Yes, boss," he chuckled. "That's that."

He swung round and rode away, grimly humming a verse of his favourite song to the old tune of "Oh, My Darling Clementine,"—

"We'll be riding where they're hiding
Any place beneath the sky—
We'll still haunt them beat and taunt them,
Till real justice can be done!"

*You'll read in next week's thrill-packed story how Trig M'fee returns to life!*

SOFTIE SIMPKINS.

NERO and ZERO The ROLLICKING ROMANS.

HAPPY HARRY — THE CAMERA MAN —

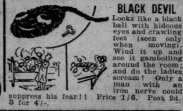

# FUN FOR ALL

**WHAT TIME IS IT?**

If four cats eat a kipper, what time is it?

12.45—a quarter (of a kipper) to one (cat).

**A CUTE TRICK.**

Can you form the letter N with three pennies? You might try a long time without managing to do it.

Have a look at the sketch to see how it's done.

**STRING 'EM.**

Get a long piece of string and ask one of your pals to catch hold of it. Tell him you can cause electricity to travel right through his body.

Now rub your hands up and down the piece of string and ask him if he can feel anything.

If he says he can't, tell him you can't do the trick without some more of your pals. Then, when you've got about six of them hanging on the string,, you simply say "I only wanted to see how many fools I could get on a piece of string."

**CHAIR FOOTBALL.**

Have you ever played chair football?

Take two chairs of the same style and place them facing each other a few yards apart.

Both you and your chum sit down on them and hold your hands so as to cover the space between the chair legs as well as possible.

One player takes a ball and tries to throw it past the other's hands into the goal.

Then the other has a try, and so the game goes on, until one or other of the players succeeds in scoring the required amount of goals needed to win the game. This, of course, is decided by the players before the game begins.

**BACK TO BACK.**

Sit down on the floor back to back with your chum, and twine your arms in his. Now both of you try to raise yourselves to your feet without letting your arms come apart.

The result is really funny, for each seems to be preventing the other from rising.

**A PRONOUNCED SUCCESS.**

Try this one on a chap who thinks no one can spring a catch on him. Pronounce ' f-o-l-k ', you say.

Now when he has done so, say "Pronounce the word for the white of an egg."

"Yolk," he will almost certainly say. How soft he'll feel when he sees his mistake.

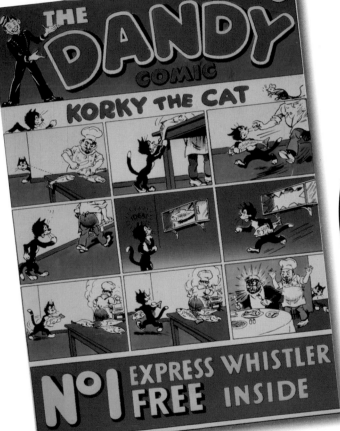

# A Merry Xmas To You All From Jock M'Dade And His Chums

Christmas comes but once a year, but the lads of Auchentogle make the most of it, and how! Jock M'Dade was feeling cheery, and he thought of a great idea. He would have an Auchentogle Christmas tree!

"Let's go round a' the mothers and faithers and get presents for the bairns," he suggested. "Then we'll hang them on a tree and present them to the kids."

The gang thought this a smart stunt, but all of them wanted to be Santa Claus.

Jock quelled the uproar with a few well-aimed cuffs on the ear.

"Which o' you lads has got a lang white beard?" he roared. "Nane o' ye! But I have!" And he produced a straggly-looking beard. He'd cut it off the milkman's billy goat, but that didn't matter. Jock was elected Santa Claus.

When the word of the Christmas tree got round, all the youngsters flocked along for their presents.

There was something for everybody – even the Auchentogle cats and dogs.

Wullie Whippet's dog got a bone, and ran off with Jock's beard. But everyone knew who Santa was anyway.

No Christmas tree is complete without a fairy. Wee Hughie got the job on Jock's tree.

He thought it was a bit of a cissy's job sitting on top of a tree, but his brother soon fixed that. He went to an upstairs window and passed over a candy-apple on a long stick to the fairy. That kept Wee Hughie quiet.

There were even carols to entertain the kids. Spud Tamson gave a few selections on his cornet. Eck Wilson didn't think much of the music.

"Gie it a drink, Spud," he said, and hurled a nice soft snowball down the open end of the cornet.

Spud carefully put down his instrument and stood Eck on his head in a snowdrift.

By this time the last of the presents had been handed out, and all the kids were showing off their new toys. Then Jock had another bright suggestion.

"Now," he said, "If ye've a' got yer ain pennies, we'll go and celebrate Christmas in the fish and chip shop." And away they went.

# THE STORY OF A GRAND NEW PICTURE BOOK

THE EDITOR AND THE ARTIST HAVE GOT READY ALL THE DRAWINGS—

—THE PRINTERS HAVE PRINTED THOUSANDS OF COPIES—

—AND THEY ARE BEING SENT TO ALL THE NEWSAGENTS' SHOPS ALL OVER THE COUNTRY!

WHIZZ

NEWSAGENT

AND THIS IS THE BOOK →

THE **BROONS** BOOK IS THE GREATEST BOOK OF PICTURES YOU EVER SAW!

IT HAS A LOVELY COLOURED COVER AND THERE ARE 128 PAGES AND EVERY PAGE IS A FULL SIZE COMIC PICTURE OF "THE **BROONS**"

LIKE THE ONE YOU SEE EVERY WEEK IN THE FUN SECTION.!!

JINGS! IT'S RARE!

THE **BROONS**

—SCOTLAND'S HAPPY FAMILY THAT MAKES EVERY FAMILY HAPPY—

FANCY ME IN A BOOK!

EVERY BOY AND EVERY GIRL IN SCOTLAND WILL WANT THIS GREAT PICTURE BOOK!

GET YOUR MA OR YOUR PA TO GO TO THE NEWSAGENT'S AND TELL HIM TO PUT YOUR NAME DOWN FOR—

"THE **BROONS**" BOOK

IT WILL BE READY FOR YOU ON FRIDAY 17th NOVEMBER.

PRICE 1/6

The first compilation of The Broons went on sale on November 17, 1939. The cover was painted by Dudley Watkins and is a fine example of his colour work, as is the cover painting for The Oor Wullie Book of 1940 on page 74.

DUDE DAWSON
BATTLING BENSON
ONE-JOINT JOHNSON
PODGE PERKINS
SLUG McCOY
LEFTY WRIGHT
NASTY JOE
LANKY LAWSON
HAMFIST HOGAN

Dudley D. Watkins produced an extraordinary volume of top class work throughout his career, never missing a deadline. His principal output was in black and white, but he had a passion for colour work and this passion was indulged in the pages of D.C.Thomson's Big Five, Rover, Wizard, Hotspur, Adventure and Skipper. This Skipper cover is an example of Watkins' early colour work.

# OOR WULLIE

OOR WULLIE, YOUR WULLIE, A'BODY'S WULLIE

# SCOTLAND'S FAVOURITE—OOR WULLIE IN A BOOK

# LOOPY LIMERICKS

There was a young fellow of Lynn
Who was so uncommonly thin
    That when he essayed
    To drink lemonade,
He slipped through the straw and
    fell in.

There was a young fellow whose feet
Were certainly not very neat.
    But as a shade from the sun
    They were simply A1,
Though quite out of place in the
    street.

A persistent young fellow of Bootle
On the flute every morning would
    tootle.
    This the neighbours annoyed,
    So they had him destroyed—
His playing was perfectly brutal.

There once was a crazy old Greek,
Who sat drinking water all week,
    And he took such a dose
    That when he arose,
He gurgled where others folks
    speak.

There was once a forest at Aintree
In which were a beech and a plane
    tree,
    An oak and a yew,
    And a chestnut or two,
But a sycamore ranked as the main
    tree.

A greedy old man of Marseilles
Was madly addicted to snails.
    He could polish off raw
    Half a dozen or more,
With pepper and salt on their tails.

A man by the name of M'Leod
By Nature was amply endowed.
    Each day his poor figure
    Grew bigger and bigger,
Far more than his waistcoat allowed.

There was a young fellow named
    Kiddle,
Who was terribly thin in the middle.
    How his head and his feet
    Ever managed to meet
Will remain an unsolvable riddle.

There was an old man of Dun D,
Who always had bloaters for T,
    He ate with great EEE
    Lots of cabbage and PPP,
And was happy. Why shouldn't he
    B ?

" Oh, doctor, I'm feeling so sore,
I've swallowed both apple and core,
    And last night, before bed,
    I'd a loaf of new bread,
Then got up and bolted the door !"

Said a highly original crow,
" If I stand in the rain I may grow,"
    In a fine pelting shower
    He remained for an hour,
Now his legs measure six feet or so.

# FUN FOR ALL

## ARE YOU "ATTRACTIVE" ?

Tell your pal that you're going to show him how much more attractive you are than he is.

Lay a cigarette card on his left hand, and, giving him a strong magnet, ask him to pick up the cigarette card with the magnet. He can't do it.

Then you put the card on your left hand, hold the magnet above it—and the card immediately jumps up and clings to the magnet. You say this proves you are much more attractive than your pal.

There is a secret behind the trick, of course. You must have a pin, or a gramophone needle, hidden in your left hand, and you place the card over this. The metal needle or pin is attracted by the magnet, and takes the card with it !

## FIGURE THIS ONE OUT !

Ask one of your pals to write down four figures in a row. Then you put a row of four figures underneath. Repeat this till you have six rows of four figures underneath each other.

Now tell your pal to add up these figures, and before he starts tell him that the answer will be 29,997. You'll be right.

The secret is that when you write down the four figures below your pal's you must see that each of yours plus the one directly above it adds up to nine. Get the idea ? Here's a sample :—

$$\begin{array}{r} 3218 \\ 6781 \\ 7110 \\ 2889 \\ 1674 \\ 8325 \\ \hline 29,997 \end{array}$$

## A CUTE TIP.

When trying to remove labels from glass, instead of wetting them and scraping them off, try this simple method.

Damp a sheet of brown paper and place it over the label. Leave it there for a few minutes, and then when you remove it you will see the label peeling off, too.

## TRICKY TRIANGLES.

Ask your pal if he can draw six triangles with six straight lines. When he's drawn dozens of figures and given it up you show him how.

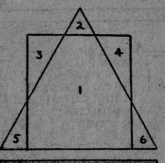

Just draw the figure...
Make the tri...
the...
...the dates all
...angles, and you will
...e a perfect square.

## THE BIG NEW COMIC'S DELICIOUS GIFT TO BOYS AND GIRLS !

# FREE WITH THE BEANO No. 2

## BIG PACKET OF SUGAR BUTTON SWEETS

Sugar Buttons Black as Jet Best You've Ever Tasted Yet

YOU GET THIS TASTY TREAT ONLY WITH No 2 OF "THE BEANO"

# ON TUESDAY 2ND AUG.

## THE BEANO'S PALS WILL MAKE YOU LAUGH !

# Ma Gets A Long Lie.

## But She Doesn't Lie Long!

# THE WAYS AND WILES O' OOR WULLIE

FAIR fa' your rosy-cheekit face,
    Your muckle buits, wi' broken lace,
Although you're always in disgrace,
    An' get your spanks,
In all our hearts ye have your place—
    Despite your pranks.

Your towsy heid, your dungarees,
Your wee snub nose, your dirty knees,
Your knack o' seeming tae displease
    Your Ma an' Pa.
We dinna care a tuppenny sneeze—
    We think you're braw.

You're wee, an' nae twa ways aboot it,
You're wise, wi' very few tae doot it,
You're wild, there's nane that wad dispute it,
    Around the toon.
But maist of a' ye are reputit—
    " A lauchin' loon."

Weel-kent, weel-liked, you're aye the same,
Tae Scots abroad and Scots at hame.
North, south, east, west, your weel-won fame
    Shall never sully.
We'll aye salute that couthie name—
    Oor Wullie.

DUDLEY D. WATKINS

# THE NEW FITBA' PITCH ON THE OLD RUBBISH DUMP

The meeting of the Auchentogle Strollers to open season 1937-38 was a great success. Jock M'Dade, of course, had to read the reports because no other body can read his writing. This is how it ran :-

"The club had a grand season in 1936-37. We won twice and were swindled in fourteen games which we lost. We reached the second round of the Fisher Cup, but were beaten 9-0, although I can say without fear of contradiction it should have been a draw.

"Unfortunately, the club secretary defunkit with the funds. But the committee will see that the same does not happen this year. They are scouting around for some suitable cripple person to whom they can safely entrust the money.

"Another tit-bit of news is that we have secured the services of an ex-Ranger to coach our players."

Loud cheers. "Wha is it?" cried Sammy Samson. "Alan Morton or Davie Meiklejohn?"

"No," replied Jock. "It's just old Jamie Tulloch, who used to be the Ranger in Auchentogle Public Park. But it looks good in writing.

"We have managed to get a new pitch on the rubbish dump," Jock went on reading. "Members are expected to turn out tomorrow night to get the pitch in order for Saturday's match. From now on the club motto will be – 'Never mind the smell, get the ba'!"

Next night the lads marked out the pitch and put up the goalposts. Spud Wilson was the head gaffer. He got Skinnymalinks Duncan, legs on him like lamp-posts, to pace out the twelve yards to the penalty spot kick, and Jock had to fight him before Spud would put the spot in its own half of the field. You see, Jock takes all the Strollers' penalties.

Sammy Samson pulled up the dandelions on the pitch. "Wonder where these roots go down to?" he gasped as he pulled. Next morning when he opened the paper he saw "Earthquake in Australia" in big type.

"I didna ken I was as strong as all that," he said, going pale.

But at ten o'clock all was ready – no tin cans on it, no broken glass, no stones, and no grass. Sammy Samson had pulled the whole twenty-five blades up because he thought they were weeds, and the pitch was all set for the grand opening game.

Auchentogle Strollers may well have had a successful opening to the 1937-38 season, but Dundee United didn't. They opened at Tannadice (shown here) against St Bernards from Edinburgh, who walloped them 7-1. United are still going strong, but St Bernards went to the dogs in 1942.

# The Broons Fair Landed In A Fix,
# When They Gaed Gaddin' Tae The "Flicks"!

SUPPLEMENT TO THE SUNDAY POST.
MAY 8, 1938.

# When The Broons Have A Holiday "Draw,"
## Everything Comes Out Right — Trust Paw!

## Aunty Bella Came To Stay.
## Maw Broon Said: " It's Been A Day!"

SUPPLEMENT TO THE SUNDAY POST JUNE 19, 1938.

# "Up In The Mornin' Early, Boys!"
## That Is The Song Paw Broon Enjoys.

## Poor Wullie's Driven Nearly Crazy.
## His Pals All Call Him "Little Daisy!"

## It Finished Daphne's Love Adventure,

## When Paw Came Asking For His Denture.

## Wullie's Palled Up With A Masher.

## He's A Society Gate-Crasher.

Hen And Joe Thought They'd Got A Couple Of "Clicks,"

Now They're After The Twins To Give Them Their Licks.

# When They Left The Coach That They'd Been Stayin' In,

## Folks Asked The Broons—Were They "In Trainin'"?

*You'll See Yourself It's No' A Haver*

*When Fouk Call Wullie " That Wee Shaver."*

**Reading was a huge part of the lives of children and adults in these pre TV 1930s days. Many bookshops dealt in second hand schoolbooks and many a queue could be seen in the days leading up to a new term.**

# JINGS! OOR JOCK'S A CLANSMAN!

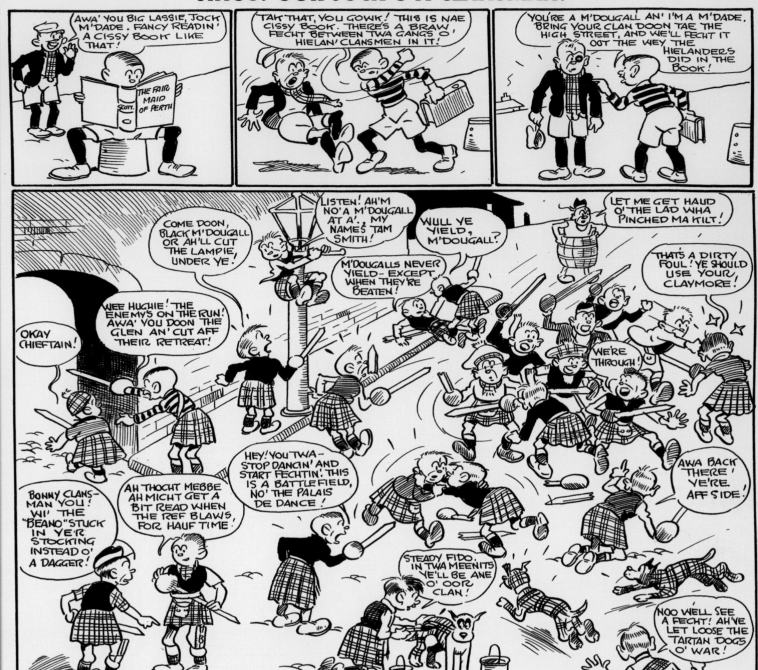

One day Jock M'Dade was peacefully reading "The Fair Maid of Perth" when Wullie M'Dougall spotted him. And Wullie called Jock a sissy for reading a novel!

So, of course, Jock gave the lad a black eye and offered to do the same for all his family and gang as well.

"Jings! A sissy book!" Jock cried. "The Hieland clans in it had a kind of a challenge match on the Inch at Perth, killing ane anither wi' claymores an' pibrochs an' a'thing! So bring oot your clan an' we'll fecht!"

Jock ordered his gang to get kilts. Where all the tartan stuff came from nobody knows, but Sammy Samson's brother is a kiltie soldier home on leave and he had to go round the town for half a day dressed in a barrel!

Jings! The two clans clashed with a noise just like Mr M'Dade breaking sticks. For the bold Highland warriors all carried wooden claymores and the air was soon thick with sawdust.

It was funny to see the clansmen stopping in the middle of a duel to sharpen their swords like pencils. But it wasn't so funny when they had to spend the whole evening picking splinters out of their ribs.

Eck Short M'Dade was put off the game. You see, Chieftain Jock nabbed him scalping a M'Dougall.

"Clansmen dinna scalp their victims!" roared Jock. "It's Red Indians that dae that! Awa' hame an' read your history!"

But, though they were a man short and though the M'Dougalls were breaking the rules by punching and using peashooters, Jock's lads drove the rival clan back.

Jock broke his sword on Wullie M'Dougall's head, stabbed him with the broken bit, jumped on his chest, and began to shout – "Say you're deid, or I'll murder you!"

Just then Kiltie M'Ara dashed into the fray to hide from his mother, who was after him for pinching the jam.

With all those kilts around, Mrs M'Ara didn't know which lad was Kiltie. So she just rang every ear in sight to make sure she got him! Mrs M'Ara's got a hand like a soup plate, so the clan fight ended in a victory for the M'Aras. By the time she had grabbed her laddie, both the M'Dades and the M'Dougalls were busy taking their sore ears home!

## Wullie Doesna Need To Sulk

## He Finds "Good Things In Little Bulk."

# Hen Gets Wilder The More He Seeks.
## He's Got A Date—He's Lost His Breeks!

## Poor Wullie's In A Hole, It's Silly,
## Especially When The Hole's In Wullie.

## Paw Broon Tries To Mend A Leak.

## He Gets His Porridge Through The Reek.

## Wullie's Full Up With Banana.

## There's Mair Tae Eat, But Wullie Canna.

# No Wonder Grandpaw's Face Is Red—
# The "Boys" have Wrecked His Cabinet Bed!

## Wullie Wanted A Day In Bed.

## Now He's Hanging A Calendar In His Shed.

# THE BROONS

D. C. THOMSON & CO. LTD.
LONDON · MANCHESTER · DUNDEE

Oor
Wullie and The Broons,
although written by the same
man, R.D.Low, and drawn by Dudley
Watkins, were very different in nature.
The Broons portrayed the family life of the
day and the humour arose from the
mundane. The genius of Watkins was
extracting humour from very ordinary
situations and he had a penchant for
creating homely, living room scenes.
There are many examples in
this book.

# Wullie Found A Curious Path

## To Lead Him To A Nice Hot Bath.

# Paw And Grandpaw At A Party —
# No Wonder Things Went Good And Hearty!

## To Make Up For Poor Santa's Shock,
## Wullie Himsel' Must Take A Knock.

# Whaur's The Broons?   Wait Till Ye See 'Em!
# They're All Locked Up In The Town Museum!

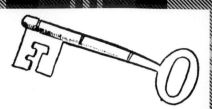

# These Pictures Prove Without A Doubt
# His Maw Kens Wullie Inside Out.

## To Play Badminton The Family's Itchin'.
## Look! They're At It In The Kitchen.

## See Wullie Now A Cowboy Fan,
## And In The End He Gets His Man.

## One Good Turn Deserves Another.
## Paw Should Have Saved Himself The Bother.

# Oor Wullie Got A Job Quite Rum.

## As Usual, He Was Not So Dumb.

## Paw And Grandpaw Look Gey Shy
## When They're Told " The Camera Cannot Lie."

# SHOCKS AT THE AUCHENTOGLE DOCKS!

Big events happen at Auchentogle Docks twice a day. That's when the tide comes in. Nothing else ever comes in there. The place couldn't harbour a grudge, though, mind you, nine years ago come next Tuesday, they once docked the harbourmaster's wages.

But Jock M'Dade and his gang sailed down there one afternoon to liven things up. They found a lot of fish in crates.

"What are they?" asked Eck Short. "Kippers before they get sunburnt?" "No," replied Jock, his brother. "They're haddocks. Folk smoke them and then they're called smokies."

"Ye dinna get me to believe that," cried Eck. "Nae man could get one of these fish in his pipe."

Those haddocks soon changed into flying fish, for the boys had a battle with them. Sammy Samson slammed Spud Wilson in the ear with one when he was fishing.

"That's a fishing smack," he cried.

But Spud Wilson sat with a face as solemn as a back door until he hauled out a flat fish. "Throw it back," cried Sammy. "The poor thing's been run over by a submarine."

Jock M'Doo was playing leap frog over the things they tie in ships to when he tramped on Dosey Tamson and knocked him into the water.

Jock has never liked Dosey, so with great presence of mind he threw him a bar of iron. But Dosey had a cake of soap in his pocket so he just washed himself ashore.

When Greedy Joe fell in the tide came in across the river. Joe can't swim, and somebody was playing with the lifebuoy. The rescue man bent his best boat-hook on Joe, and had given him up for lost. But Jock M'Dade saved him by shouting, "Here's the slider man, Joe."

Jock says that Joe just got up and ran over the water. Anyway he was safe on the side in two ticks.

Sandy M'Nab has exploring blood in him and he built a raft. "They've discovered the North Pole and the South Pole, but me and Ecky Drumtochty's going to sail to the West Pole," he said.

The voyage was never started. Mr M'Nab and the rest of the fathers came on the scene to collect their sons.

"Ah'll gie you Docks," was all the lads heard at bedtime. But they were up to their tricks by the next morning.

# Now, Folks, You Should Hear Wullie Say—

## "It Pays To Pass The Time Away."

## Their Music Was More Than Paw Could Stand,
## But In The End Paw " Beat The Band."

# *Wullie Has Noted In His Book,*

## *Folks Are Not Always What They Look.*

*The Scottish Beat The English Broon,*

*But The Referee Was A Forfar Loon.*

# Wull Gave The Champ The K.O., True,
# But You Can't Knock Spots Off A Kangaroo.

## When The Broons Ask Family Friends To Tea,

## It's Mair Like A Sunday School Soiree.

## "HI, WANT HALF A CROWN?"—

### OOR WULLIE'S GIVING THEM AWAY FREE!

From Jedburgh to John o' Groats, from Aberdeen to Ardnamurchan, boys and girls are writing in to tell Oor Wullie what's interesting about the place they live in. Why not write and tell Oor Wullie where you live? Half a crown will be awarded _____ of every _____

### CULROSS.

IF you were to come to Culross, near where I live, and look out across the Firth of Forth, you would see, a short distance from the shore, a little island with some ruined buildings on it — they are the buildings around the pit-shaft of what was probably Scotland's first coal-mine!

During the sixteenth century, this mine, which was dug a mile under the Firth, was one of the greatest wonders in Scotland. And in 1617 James the Sixth is said to have paid it a visit.

He was taken down the shaft on the shore and after going through the mine he was brought up on the little island.

When the King saw water all around him, he thought he had been trapped.

"Treason! Treason!" he cried, but the people with him soon convinced him that he was safe, and he was taken ashore in a boat. The mine was destroyed by a terrible storm in March 1625.

Margaret Rennie, Shiresmill, Newmills, by Culross.

### NEWBURGH.

NEWBURGH is the place I live in. It is a town standing on one bank of the Tay nearly twenty miles from its mouth.

Perhaps the most interesting thing in Newburgh is the Macduff Cross which is at least six hundred years old. It used to bear an inscription which has baffled experts for centuries.

The number nine plays a big part in the stories about the cross. It is said that the base of the cross used to contain **nine** rings, and any of the clan Macduff who had committed a crime could seek sanctuary there by grabbing one of the rings.

Then his crime would be pardoned if he washed himself **nine** times at the cross and paid a fine of **nine** cows by tying them to the rings. The washing was done at a spring which is still called **Nine** Wells!

Hugh Cairncross, 133 High Street, Newburgh, Fife.

I LI__ D __ bank Stirling __ small, __ is a very interesting place.

To the south-east of the town lies the Tor Wood, which is a remnant of the ancient Caledonian Forest which used to stretch over the greater part of Scotland. It was in the leafy branches of an oak tree in this wood that William Wallace once sought refuge while being hounded by his enemies.

__ the __ with __ gorge where __ Randolph leaped to her death while trying to escape her pursuers. The place is now called the Lady's Leap.

In the same glen can be seen a huge boulder resting in the branches of a tree. The rock is much too big for anyone to lift, yet there it sits jammed high up in that tree! How did it manage to get there? Nobody seems to know.

Betty Ferguson, 64 Dryburgh Avenue, Denny.

# THE MAGIC COMIC

Nº 1 · 22ND JULY · 1939
EVERY THURSDAY
2D

## KOKO THE PUP

FULL OF TRICKS AND FULL OF FUN. KOKO'S A PAL FOR EVERYONE!

# PETER PIPER

## PICKING PEOPLE OUT OF PICKLES

Beside the statues in the park
Walks Peter Piper, a bright spark.
But Peter's due some nasty shocks,
For two toughs wait to give him socks.

Pete passes by   The bullies pounce!
His chin upon the ground they bounce,
And tug his hair and pull his ears—
But help's at hand, so dry your tears!

For, hearing all the sounds of strife,
A stony statue wakes to life!
It's Pan the Piper, and he wipes
His eyes—then tootles on his pipes!

His music rings out wild and clear
And—look out, kids!  What have we here?
To life the Samson statue wakes!
With rage and wrath he simply quakes.

He throws the stone with all his might
And gives the bullies such a fright
That Peter now can dodge away—
Then Samson leaps into the fray!

The tough guys think they're in a war,
For Samson gives them both what for!
And meanwhile Pan jumps to his feet
And gives his set of pipes to Pete.

"One toot—and statues wake!" says he.
And while the yelling bullies flee,
Young Peter tootles—"Roo-too-too!"
To see if what Pan says is true.

It works!  For Cupid, full of go,
Fits two stone arrows to his bow.
Then—twang!  The archer's aim is good.
He's punctured both the bullies rude!

Back in their place the statues stand.
You'd think they'd never moved a hand.
But pipeless Pan is winking now.
Will Pete have fun?  He will—and how!

Next Thursday Peter's hard to beat—He makes stone statues clean the street!

Once again the prolific Watkins featured in a new publication. These Peter Piper strips are examples of his work of that period. The strip on the left contains Peter Piper, or is it Oor Wullie? The strip above contains a character with a startling resemblance to a resident of Bunkerton Castle, a certain Lord Snooty.

# When Daphne Had The Bridesmaid's Place,
## She Had A Job To Save Her Face.

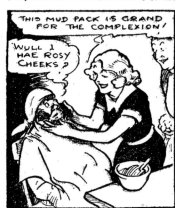

# The Family All Thought A Lot
# O' The Job That Daphne Never Got.

SUPPLEMENT TO THE SUNDAY POST, SEPTEMBER 10, 1939.

War was declared on Sunday, September 3, 1939 and one week later, both strips had a wartime theme, testament to just how current the themes were, and still are.

Many towns and cities around Britain were targets for the German bombers, and to reduce the danger of damage and injury from bomb blasts, buildings were sandbagged. This photograph shows the D.C.Thomson building in Dundee and the measures taken to keep Oor Wullie and The Broons mercilessly lampooning the Axis leaders for the ensuing six years.

*Although It Wasna' At The Start,*

*The Cuddy's Properly " In The Cart."*

The Broons, oor ain sort o' folk,
Good fir a smile an' a joke.

See thon Wullie, the cheeky chappie,
He's a laugh and keeps us happy.

**Have a laugh with Oor Wullie and The Broons every week in**

# The SUNDAY POST

The archive nature of the material in this book means that image quality may vary slightly throughout. Some pages may contain references which are of their time, but would not be considered suitable today.